Escape Artist

Vivian Moon

BookLeaf
Publishing

Escape Artist © 2022 Vivian Moon

All rights reserved.

No part of this publication may be reproduced, stored in a retrieval system, or transmitted, in any form or by any means, electronic, mechanical, photocopying, recording or otherwise, without the prior written permission of the presenters.

Vivian Moon asserts the moral right to be identified as author of this work.

Presentation by *BookLeaf Publishing*

Web: www.bookleafpub.com

E-mail: info@bookleafpub.com

ISBN: 9789357695879

First edition 2022

This book of poems is dedicated to my family who's given me the opportunity to pursue my goals wholeheartedly. To my partner who teaches me how to love myself as much as I love others. To my friends who create on their own terms & persevere with heart and integrity.

Pursuit

Turns out I've been keeping my art covered
strange entrance to recover
white walls like high brow
did not come from the streets or my lovers.
I am inspired by my mother
and other women.
Man, did I stutter?
You and me are not the same
but anytime I open eyes mouth
write in open range
we're not contained by our backgrounds or
biases
not our faces but I still feel conspired against
hard to trust
after dreaming of snakes
feeling the outcomes of snakes
the clash of friends who got different shit to
stake
while here I am to isolate.
That's how I learned.
The wild women are overturned when we keep
making excuses
talking to our urn.
I will never accept defeat
not from love list or what comes easy

because some routes come easy
and I can sometimes be lazy
learning now to refresh and sleep so it's clear not hazy
energy regained so I can figure out what phased me
how I want to place me my product and service on the map
where I'll start and who I'll attract.
I am no speakeasy hidden corner.
I do not speak easy each essence makes me feel like a coroner.
Any word is danger so I'll string them up like orders.
Death doesn't hold back the comic or the poet.
In fact, it raises up the stakes for us natural mourners
lords of domain to be remembered by the loyal but nobody is loyal.
We are all on our own trip passage of convinced
and I have been convinced now en route to creating ways
to make it stick and move to pursue my win.

The Concept of Containing Art

The concept of containing art.
I am not a structure intended
to stay on stage coming apart
or coming together,
coming at all.
I'm not a voice to be carried through,
the impact troupe,
have sat in too many
no such thing
underground bars and roofs,
dark rooms where you see people
who stopped grooming
those leaking their needs
some soothing.
At times I feel nude,
coated in layers
but my chills find me regardless.
Must be the cold offsetting my harvest
enriched by the heat the sun and
nights in solitude.
My attitude can keep me from seeing,
so I write endlessly sometimes
but right now it's a struggle
to combat my own rebuttal

of what I've been doing
and what the future needs
beyond our struggle as artists,
conceptual farcists.
I am not fake,
just craving out of this box
I call it clout
shout.
You say bars like it's not keeping me out.
I call this no dilemma,
a planning phenomenon
to uncage
uprise and
start.

Dear God I pray for those broke

Dear god, I pray for all of those broke.
No system could save lack of savings.
Man, that's a joke.
One the system begets to let the front-line choke,
not enough supplies so we watch behind closed
doors
separated
paranoia.
The study of self got me woke.
Our own actions whose actions could profit from
mishandling,
if that's in fact what corruption proposed.
You hear it over and over.
That's the science of illusory truth.
How can we stop the image if we're pulled by
the roots?
Our goodness cut back to make room for
disinfectant
survival instinct.
Watch who's got the competitive advantage.
Watch who makes moves for the
disenfranchised.
Watch those sectors that turn a blind eye
infuse us with blindness:

rabid consumption of
supposed refinement.
Who can sacrifice when we're just tryna eat?
Who can turn time when history repeats?
All I know is where there's fat, there is meat.
And when there's no hope, all I had to do was
turn the cheek.
Never mind the bullshit speech or the sponsored
meme.
Harnessing energy for salvation toward the
green.
What curiosity breeds can invoke a masterpiece.

To Escape

To escape is not to mourn or
scorn over what's been done.
Escape is releasing the fixtures and the sum.
What once contained can now run
without hold or decree.
Truth shall be set free
from the mind of Thich Nhat Hanh
and Causmosis.
Life is but a play or dream.
What have you dreamed?
Maybe a freedom that here seems obscene:
choosing me over man
soul over CREAM
self over family
Now that's prognosis.
To escape is a notion
of mentality.

If I won't swallow the pill

If I won't swallow the pill
and don't ever conform
why do I resist
breaking out of the norms
completely?
Don't need salvation
from screens or likes
want to make an impact
reach for what
but there's a price.
I know where my heart lies.
It's real and comes easy.
Poems on lips say
they need me
so I spit and believe
that we've come.
No, not sleazy.
Delivered once and
we're breathing
Still alive
see
even when deceived
even if it's right or not
it's not mine
nor will it serve me.

So I honor my essence
and speak.

Social Experiment

Just imagine for a second
that we're not robots
programmed by unnecessary
reliance on products
to make the people we hate rich,
programmed by algorithms
to take our ability to think
quick or slow for our growth
and have a healthy debate
and dialogue in the flow.
That's what lip service did.
Licked lips like woke tastes good,
even on hypocrites.

I am no villain
no sacrificial meat
chopped on the wood
as if I dont need to eat
breathe.
The work was done by you and me.
No one deserves this.
Truth is we earned it.
Tech started to save us
then greed adjusted to divert it.
Diversity became a statement

thread with common thought.
I dare you to put us again in a box.
Keep talking to ourselves in the mirror
that caught the image.
We'd rather pillage the enemy named
instead of naming the fear,
stuck statements,
or circular reasoning.
Tell me the difference between
conversation and thrust
opinions without trust of return.
Been robbed so long,
we'd rather watch the shit burn.

-

Dear God, I've been struggling to live
true to my essence so God please forgive.
Pray for the sins that literally made me sick.
Soul from mind manipulated.
You might say that's tricks.
Was this always normal? Fighting for our rights.
Last I checked, I was born and given life.
Don't tell me we didn't fight for peace &
dignity.
That's why we sharpen the knife.

-

So why do we pay taxes for carefully crafted lies
with focus on greed as if children are the price?
More debt that crept up
when the impact is how we treat others
and ourselves but here & now
we hardly bother.
See a cause in the name.
Causmosis works to end that lame
box because we've been squared up.
No wonder we feel attacked,
swinging hatred like that's what we're made of.
Pure souls are not rare,
just hard to excavate
Requires mining of the mind
push past whats engrained.
That's hate hurt lessons learned
burned so we stop yearn for peace
comfort in lessons we know
and opinions we agree with.
Mind the grievance.
How will we receive it?

There's a reason why shit is politicized,
turns our humanity to a tool to divide
and when there's division,
the trolls take power
advantage of our place.
We are not evil
so let facts dictate and know

psychology is in PLAY.
That's what we grew up in!
Society's been incessant and immoral.
That's what we can claim
with no debate
as much as self-hate
they've been trying to engrain for profit.

I wasn't raised to assimilate with the violence.
Hold up, I was trained to assimilate with the violence.
Blast the American Dream or rather the pilot,
a social experiment for colonizer's creed.
Chase that money/grind.
Put in a language to relate to you and me.
Labeled outsider from the ones who hold the key
yet do not claim us.
The social experiment... betrayed us.

What's the line?

What's the line?
Give me a sign. Have they been reprimanded
for the evils that resign some to the level of
mime
not people mere votes to deny
What's the line?
We been resigned to following lines.
The world that we live in want to swallow and
sigh
performing antics
distracting the pawns
so we don't get along
What's the line?
A statement or mission printed in submission
to corporate responsibility
like gears in mechanic function
What's the line?
Subtext.
Stress the policy.
Which flex will be stylish on me.
Comfort is not free and appropriation is cheap
What's the line?
Bordering the benefits that I receive
stimulus package stealing access to BC
from Medicaid enrollees but that we don't see

What's the line?
Connected in fashion
tech and memes yet we don't see
AG sweeping powers manipulating screens.
FCC stole net neutrality 2018
What's the line?
The lien
the debt that we pay
as US dollar recedes.
Plant the seeds to guarantee survival.
Power in supply and community
What's the line?
Life lines got us prying for sanity or saving.
The fear is ingratiating caught up on sides
when we could be raising minds
instead lies. The data's been comprised
Whats the line?

Void

I'm pulled back into the void
don't hear music or the noise.
Maybe an echo from dimensions far away
in time and space or mind states.
Fair play or is that too much to ask for in the void?
When pulled from conversations out of noise
where you're like what am I saying why am I here?
Can I please get another beer?

Brainwash

It's the brainwash talking! Rinse and repeat.
Think you're blocking but its lather suds
distracting blocking vision. Don't hear revisions
simple directions believe the weather, as if it's
laid out on backs as if truth is the goal. Damn
we've been played South turning brains
remnants of schools waned off facts and science
to trends. Who'll buy it?! Simply business.
Grind is the goal. Entrepreneurs make the world
run or sold. That's innovation yet studies focus
on gold. Stimulation yet we focus on the mold
the image of what we can must pillage stuck in
the rinse cycle of stifled crimp and style
mishandled into triptych of which potential
disaster. Wash sins off like Hieronymus Bosch
laughter fallen angel but it's just plaster. Statues
looming taking over so I'll just say No Idols!

I miss the park

I miss the park
the days when life was great picking at bark
What's under the layers?
Curiosity still an art
Just now there are to-dos and do-nots
Sky's blue so fear not
Rules and regulations
to fit the farce
do not appease me
Nuanced believing
swore it would not be easy
Hands out so we retrieve
what's given.
I trust the rhythm
patterns of tricks
cycles with wits
Sometimes can't trust my guts for shit
Sometimes facts distract from systems
so switch them around
to compound the scene.
What do you see?
Miss days in the park
where living is easy

Life is but a dream

Life is but a dream and the scene is fresh
No debate allowed, only love and sess
The point of acceptance is also happiness
Don't follow the crowd or you'll get lost in it
That's where I find myself this day, this month
Unbearable warmth to heavens above
but hold up, I haven't made it there yet
Still reaching out trying to grab at my threads
when all that needs grabbing is the heart
This zone is not made for tv screens or even phones
My finesse is rocks and stones
stargazing alone, until someone can join me.
This life is not hard. It's confusing
makes people like me double back and contemplate
analyze why or how I live that way
Do I really have needs that require living in dreams?
Apparently, if there's any amount of freedom
but see that may be another fallacy
Another agreement another shell I saw and claimed and conquered
called it my own and signed resigned
put up my crimes and defined accordingly

I am not a hermit crab so why am I feeling like one?
My shell is but a mirage but the paradise is beyond
skin and bones or thrones
It's free fall.

I want to get away

I want to get away
 reach for better days
as if isolation could cure me,
depths secured.
Inevitable is lonely.
Still I reach,
dont want phonies,
no mirage or illusion,
not from them or me.
What does it look like to be free?
Not incessantly charming,
words off lips not alarming,
in fact frozen from the cold maintained,
distance saves,
so how much further do we go to pray?

Coffee and Muffin

This morning I've got freestyles running in my mouth along with coffee and delicious banana chocolate chip muffin. My rhymes don't stop or s(h)it in my mouth! Chalk it up to raise wealth anytime as my own, so I don't let the moments loose blown out of my hands. I've got a handle, so don't block my sun or my plans. I'm awake not baked clear headed with the risk of one alcoholic take. Last night embedded. Possible head(aches). But I still woke up indebted to the great weather. Cool at last! My favorite season is here so we can fall with class. Fall out of needs to please or interact surface level without love intact. Yes, I love strangers and could have shared more. But I can't defend the world if I can't defend myself. Lots of thoughts running coming out of fingertips like thundering. God must feel this way when the rain pours and Earth is rumbling.

Starving

I'm starving
for lunch
breakfast
a break
from the incessant pull
of what I've got to do
but what is it I got to do
if not meant for me?
Just want to share my truth
and bump this beat
and write poems that
make your hearts skip.
This bears repeating every couple years
seems its fleeting.
My conviction solid when I'm fed
not depleting.
Pursuing more than images
This is breathing.
This is hip hop
arts and culture
as the world flops
commenting on more
than message boards
of mind-full hoards
trying to meditate

and I've been saved.
Five minutes every day
work miracles like naivete.
It'll all work out – that's what we've got to say
but I'm from the school
where its ok to throw rules out
if there's clout,
principles to shout or demonstrate,
counteraction to exist,
not just to stay.
 I'm starving.
Who's ready to penetrate
these walls
Who's ready to overturn these brawls
into a better state?
Defined by basic needs met
like fruit bowls over microwave.
Nix mind control - we need to cultivate.
Voting this year?
Mind over matter but you don't matter?
That's a scandal insinuated by hopeless digestion
survival in question
but some hierarchy of needs
been stuck on systems.
Our higher beings been reminiscing
and I'm reaching for a plate in this discussion.

Pulse

I felt the pulse between my brows as they hit surround sound, merely a witness as I shake off the crown and materials. The feeling is ephemeral, doesn't last. The world today moves fast but do we keep up or merely pay to last in relevance? My heart is steadfast, resilient, yet my brain and bones aching to stand up say no because it's evident - I do not belong in this world. Sometimes wish I could accept but my soul says resist. I will not be kept - the power is in words, not fists. I am the wind, not a rose or a kiss, not properly packaged for the next deal or dismiss. I am peace on the cusp, a movement full of us or at least the consciousness. Dark times have allotted this and, as many of us are trained to take hits, being the bigger person might just be focusing on that sweet abyss.

When I was young

When I was young stayed in a closet dreamed of what happiness could be. Goals. Set out to break the mold while simultaneously held like stone in the image. Good daughter. Good attributes. Great legacy. Ain't that the truth? So great it fed the lions and cracked the hooves so no wild could leave the room.

Sat in a closet, wrote about the logic of writing, how I could escape and no one around me could flag it. Became enigmatic convinced. I was neither a dream or a fix. I was mine, back into the holes gaps of time. Pressures don't reside, instead reject any and all thoughts crept via other holds on stones, tried to stone and not condone. Such hate still resides in those roles meant to uplift, caught in a job or dare I say, a crypt. Anything to avoid the young hearts in the void that is cultural programming or corporate ladder. Wait for the selfie or shooting to make it sadder.

When I was young stayed in a closet wrote endlessly wreaking havoc thinking that's all it could be to make me happy and some would say that's tragic.

When the world stops and stares

When the world stops and stares,
what do you do?
Will you pose, flash a smile
and propose a plan
or make a toast
or will it be a look up
from distracted states
like what'd I say?
No memory of strategies
to play the game
can save us.
Photographer-for-hire
may despise us
when the world stops
heavy
finally
with the load of
unanswered questions,
though there will still be
propositions and sales.
When money fails
and screens unfold
as if the story lived in hearts,
not noses up

or in celebrity whims
or stalker games
or TV once called a win.
What will you do then?

Insomnia

I'm seeking perspective at 6 am. My last draft went dead with my computer clamped shut. My hope for salvation through poem shattered. My own doing of course barely feel remorse. Still seeking saving in my notes wondering how much cosmos can save me in full force of my waking death. Insomnia pet. I am owned by never ending dread of what must be done has to be kept in lines. I tried to make sense before it rhymed and still find my mind in its depths. These poems have saved me and yet they make it so hard to rest.

Do what I can

I do what I can, every inch or piece. Send me a prayer so I can eat become nurtured not sweeped like debris, treated like a percentage of the dollar. They want me to stay leashed like on collar, and who is they, they becoming us when retrained to self-prophesize our lust. Must we pray for a salvation through cuts, budgets bust, no trust in systems, lip services the customs. Manuscripts must speak the truth but anyone can write a book or run for office with a noose. I contribute & go figure if we'll lose. That's hope for the best and expect the worst. Combined with pride and ego, "to do" could be a curse.

Unlearning

Assimilated to the violence
blindness of our inputs
and consequences as culprits.
A system is an inter-related
and automatic sequence
of parts & in the design,
we each play a role.
Focus on your lane
- the notion told to bestow
self-hatred self-limits.
Internalize the blame so
instead of change,
we seek to soothe.
My peace recently recovered
from an insolent snooze
put on by who.
It all takes work whether
with tears or a bruise.
We've been abused dissected
still persevere undetected
for the timely recluse.
Time has come through
to shed light bared tonight
in principles that make you.

Bear down for your unlearning
(that means finding your happiness too)
Beyond ads or prior hurt
paid off or going berserk
from constant denial and destruction
presented as improvement.
Must regain retain and regrow
before we fall victim to our
holy habits short memory.
Goal is to seek third eye for recovery.
Head aches from exposure
constant to screens
news bombarded with
what to think and how
written by who what how?
When expertise lies,
try to come up for air.
Remember our awakening
doesn't equate to impactful action.
It takes questions and trips down conversations
that may make your head split.
Been strict unkind understanding
so I won't be underhanding my principles.
Are we guilty if we settle with what's
comfortable?
I move and pray to act on what I say,
grateful for the people
who gave me the patience to say
I DISAGREE!

That's a blessing.
Only way to grow is a hard-earned lesson.
Unlearning is the answer, not the question.

Grew Up

Grew up in a bubble
negative rebuttals
so I see in you what I see in me
Remnants of a framed society
cut and soddered to become
sons and daughters
of a machine

Grew up troubled
seeing Queens in you and me
as structures attempted to silence
predicted violence
No thread of preventative care
They said be aware
and stay in kindness

Grew up eyes open
in solitary confinement
felt the need to escape
home towns and voices aligned with
principles like profit
reputation in pockets
What was mine
systems claimed it theirs

Grew up turned down
so focus was the crown
third eye before any trend or label
rather not call it stable
grew skin thick like my hair
and my brows.
Spoke loud
especially when they didn't want me to.
Silence was the absolute curse:
to be caught submissive
in my heart or thirst.

Grew up wanting more with less
and confess that all I wanted
was happiness.

Printed in the USA
CPSIA information can be obtained
at www.ICGtesting.com
LVHW011141120424
777206LV00016B/1342